Who Was
George Washington?

WASHINGTON

Who Was
George Washington?

By Roberta Edwards
Illustrated by True Kelley

Grosset & Dunlap

GROSSET & DUNLAP
Published by the Penguin Group
Penguin Group (USA) Inc., 375 Hudson Street, New York, New York 10014, USA
Penguin Group (Canada), 90 Eglinton Avenue East, Suite 700, Toronto,
Ontario M4P 2Y3, Canada (a division of Pearson Penguin Canada Inc.)
Penguin Books Ltd., 80 Strand, London WC2R 0RL, England
Penguin Group Ireland, 25 St. Stephen's Green, Dublin 2, Ireland
(a division of Penguin Books Ltd.)
Penguin Group (Australia), 250 Camberwell Road, Camberwell, Victoria 3124, Australia
(a division of Pearson Australia Group Pty. Ltd.)
Penguin Books India Pvt. Ltd., 11 Community Centre, Panchsheel Park,
New Delhi—110 017, India
Penguin Group (NZ), 67 Apollo Drive, Rosedale, North Shore 0632, New Zealand
(a division of Pearson New Zealand Ltd.)
Penguin Books (South Africa) (Pty.) Ltd., 24 Sturdee Avenue,
Rosebank, Johannesburg 2196, South Africa

Penguin Books Ltd, Registered Offices: 80 Strand, London WC2R 0RL, England

Text copyright © 2009 by Grosset & Dunlap.
Illustrations copyright © 2009 by True Kelley.
Cover illustration copyright © 2009 by Nancy Harrison.
All rights reserved. Published by Grosset & Dunlap,
a division of Penguin Young Readers Group,
345 Hudson Street, New York, New York 10014.
GROSSET & DUNLAP is a trademark of Penguin Group (USA) Inc.
Printed in the U.S.A.

Library of Congress Control Number: 2008022377

ISBN 978-0-448-44892-3   10 9

Contents

Who Was
George Washington?

1783

After seven long years of fighting, the war was finally over. American soldiers had beaten the mighty British army. The thirteen colonies were independent now.

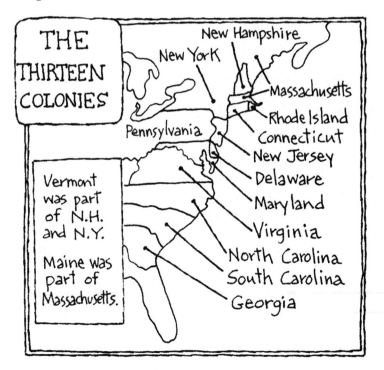

THE THIRTEEN COLONIES

New Hampshire
New York
Massachusetts
Rhode Island
Connecticut
New Jersey
Delaware
Maryland
Virginia
North Carolina
South Carolina
Georgia
Pennsylvania

Vermont was part of N.H. and N.Y.

Maine was part of Massachusetts.

Ships full of British soldiers sailed back to England. From here on in, nobody in America had to obey King George. There was going to be a brand-new country with thirteen united states.

And in 1789 when it came time to elect the first president, who was the number-one choice?

George Washington, of course.

George Washington had been the top general throughout the war. He was not the kind of general who just gave orders and then watched soldiers do the fighting; he was often in the thick of battle. Yet Washington was never wounded, not once! Besides being brave, he was also smart, loyal, honest, and fair—everything a leader should be. Would the war have been won without him? Many people didn't think so.

It was no surprise that he won the first election for president. But when he learned the news, he was not happy. Oh, no. He wasn't happy at all. He loved being back in Virginia, at Mount Vernon,

THE MOUNT VERNON HOUSE

his beautiful home. He was fifty-seven years old and hoped to spend the rest of his life there with his wife, Martha, and her two youngest grandchildren.

As the very first president, so much would be expected of him. And strange as it may seem to us, George Washington worried that he wasn't up to the job.

No, the job of president was not at all to his liking.

But many people said they would only support the new government if George Washington were president. And more than anything, he wanted the new government to work.

So he said yes and started off for New York, where he would take the oath of office.

A PARTY IN TRENTON, NEW JERSEY

At every stop along the way, there were parties and parades for him. Just what George didn't want.

Today politicians may spend years planning to run for president. Millions of dollars are spent on campaigns. Yet the man who is known as "the father of our country" felt like "a criminal going off to his execution." All he wanted was to stay home and go fox hunting!

Chapter 1
A Boy from Virginia

On the night of February 22, 1732, Augustine Washington sat at a table by candlelight. A family Bible lay open before him. Gus, as everyone called him, was a tobacco farmer in the colony of Virginia. With a pen made from the quill of a turkey, he wrote down the name of his son—George—who had been born that very morning.

George's mother, Mary, was Gus's second wife. (His first wife had died, leaving him with two teenage sons.) One night not long before George was born, a bolt of lightning shot down the chimney of the Washingtons' farmhouse. It killed a woman who was visiting Mary. Mary worried that the lightning was a sign of bad luck. It might mean that there'd be something wrong with her baby. But George was a strong, healthy baby. People said he looked like his mother. He grew into a tall, athletic boy who loved to ride horses through the green countryside. In later years he was known as the best horseman in Virginia.

FERRY FARM

When George was about seven, the family moved to Ferry Farm. It was across the river from Fredericksburg, Virginia. By this time George had a younger sister, Betty, and three younger brothers—Samuel, John, and Charles. (People said George and Betty looked a lot alike. As a grown woman, she would do funny imitations of her famous brother!)

There isn't any information about how George and his father got along. But we do know he wasn't close to his mother. Mary Washington was a cold, bossy woman. All George's friends were scared of her. Strangely, she never took pride in

A FAMOUS LIE

MANY GENERATIONS OF SCHOOLCHILDREN LEARNED THE STORY OF GEORGE WASHINGTON CHOPPING DOWN A CHERRY TREE ON HIS FAMILY'S FARM. WHEN HIS ANGRY FATHER ASKED WHO HAD DONE SUCH A TERRIBLE THING, GEORGE CONFESSED RIGHT AWAY. "I CANNOT TELL A LIE," HE SAID. "PA, IT WAS I WHO CHOPPED IT DOWN." THE STORY SHOWED HOW HONEST GEORGE WAS, EVEN AS A SMALL BOY.

THE STORY, HOWEVER, WAS ENTIRELY MADE UP.

SOON AFTER WASHINGTON'S DEATH, A MAN NAMED MASON LOCKE WEEMS WROTE A BOOK ABOUT THE FIRST PRESIDENT. WEEMS WANTED WASHINGTON TO SEEM PERFECT. AND SO HE MADE UP STORIES SUCH AS THE ONE ABOUT THE CHERRY TREE. IT TOOK MORE THAN A HUNDRED YEARS BEFORE THE TRUTH CAME OUT ABOUT THE UNTRUTHFUL BOOK.

George's Mother

her eldest son, not even after he became president. His letters to her would begin "Honored Madam" instead of "Dear Mother." And he never introduced his wife, Martha, to her!

The person he loved best in the world was his kind half-brother Lawrence. Lawrence was Gus's oldest son. He was fourteen years older than George. Lawrence had gone to school in England. He had learned Greek and Latin. He knew how to dress like a gentleman and act like a gentleman.

There wasn't enough money to send George off to England. Instead, he was taught at home, probably by his father and Lawrence. George was great at math. Anything with numbers

Lawrence Washington, George's half-brother

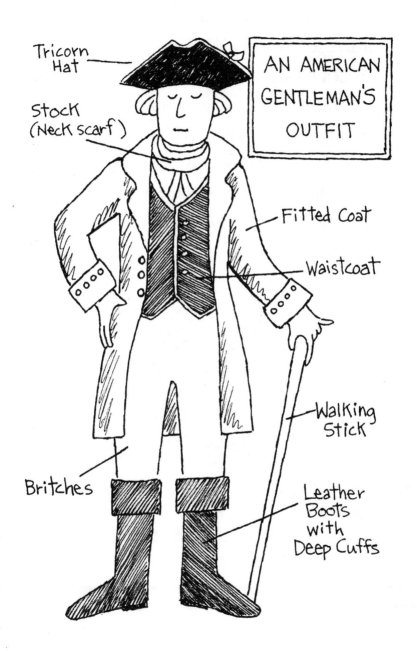

Tricorn Hat

Stock
(Neck scarf)

AN AMERICAN GENTLEMAN'S OUTFIT

Fitted Coat

Waistcoat

Walking Stick

Britches

Leather Boots with Deep Cuffs

came easily to him. But he was a terrible speller. It embarrassed him all his life.

When George was only eleven, his father died. From time to time, George was invited for long visits to Mount Vernon. This was the home of Lawrence and his new bride, Ann Fairfax. George loved it there. In 1746, George was asked to move in for good. And off he went. (He probably was happy, too, to get away from his mother!)

The Washington Family Coat of Arms. The Latin motto means "the outcome justifies the deed."

Chapter 2
Mount Vernon

At Mount Vernon a whole new world opened up for George. Now he mixed with the richest families in Virginia; he went fox hunting and to fancy balls. Shy and a little awkward, George wanted to fit in very badly. So he took dancing lessons. (In time he became an excellent dancer.)

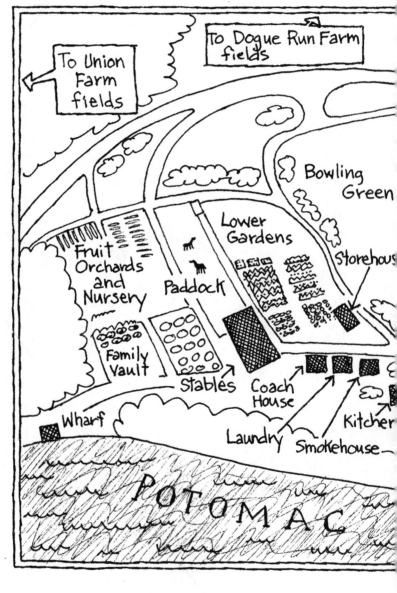

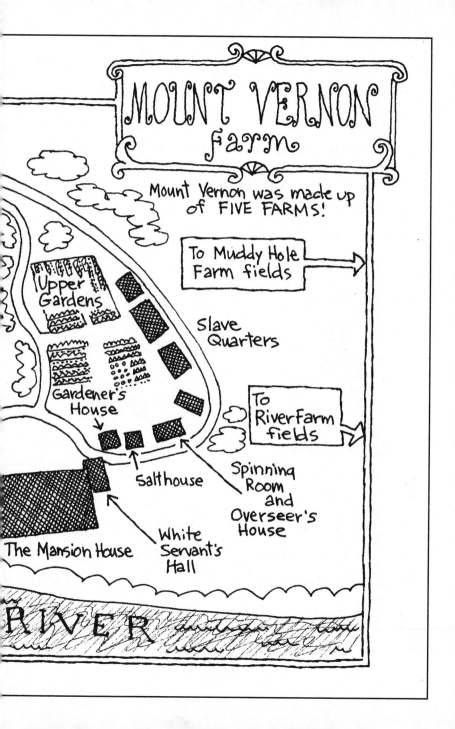

George took fencing lessons and learned about music. He wore nicer clothes. He also wrote himself a long list of rules about good manners. One of the rules was about not spitting into a fire while meat was being cooked in it! Another rule was to avoid killing fleas and lice in the presence of other people.

Lawrence's in-laws, the Fairfaxes, were one of the richest families in Virginia. They owned huge tracts of land. There were no maps yet of the west part of the colony. So people often hired surveyors.

A surveyor's job was to measure and mark property boundaries. It was the perfect job for George. He loved the outdoors, was quick at math, and needed to earn money.

Besides no maps, there were no roads in western Virginia. It was wilderness. So as a surveyor George lived a rough life. For weeks on end he'd wear the same clothes, sleep on the ground along with other hired men, cook over an open fire, and try to steer clear of hostile bands of Indians.

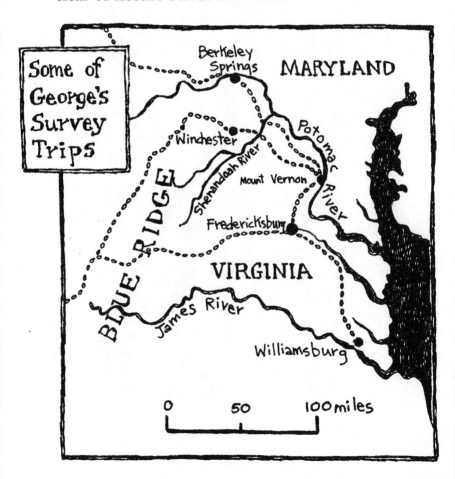

Some of George's Survey Trips

Berkeley Springs

MARYLAND

Winchester

Potomac River

Shenandoah River

Mount Vernon

Fredericksburg

VIRGINIA

BLUE RIDGE

James River

Williamsburg

0   50   100 miles

FALSE TEETH

EVEN AS A YOUNG MAN, GEORGE HAD PROBLEMS WITH HIS TEETH. THEY CAUSED HIM A GREAT DEAL OF PAIN. BY THE TIME HE BECAME PRESIDENT, HE HAD ONLY ONE REAL TOOTH LEFT. HE HAD TO WEAR FALSE TEETH.

THERE ARE STORIES ABOUT A SET OF WASHINGTON'S TEETH BEING MADE OUT OF WOOD. BUT THAT ISN'T TRUE. MOST OFTEN IVORY FROM ELEPHANTS, HIPPOS, AND OTHER ANIMALS WAS USED. THE TEETH WERE SET INTO A METAL BASE WITH HEAVY SPRINGS. NOT ONLY PAINFUL TO WEAR, THE FALSE TEETH MADE IT DIFFICULT TO EAT. THEY PUSHED OUT HIS LIPS IN AN UNNATURAL WAY THAT EMBARRASSED WASHINGTON. NO WONDER PAINTINGS OF GEORGE WASHINGTON AS AN OLDER MAN NEVER SHOW HIM SMILING!

ONE SET OF WASHINGTON'S FALSE TEETH IS DISPLAYED AT MOUNT VERNON. IT'S ONE OF THE MOST POPULAR EXHIBITS.

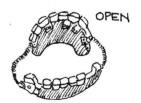
OPEN

CLOSED

George grew to be a broad-shouldered young man, with clear blue-gray eyes and reddish-brown hair. He wore it in a ponytail. At six foot two, he was often the tallest person in a group. His hands and feet were huge. Except for his bad teeth, he was in excellent health.

Lawrence, unfortunately, had much more serious health problems. He developed a terrible cough. In the hope that warm weather might help his brother, George and Lawrence sailed to the island of Barbados, off Venezuela. It was George Washington's first—and only—trip outside North America.

Sadly, Lawrence's health did not improve. And George came down with smallpox, another deadly disease. George survived; Lawrence, however, died in 1752, with George at his bedside. It was a terrible blow for George. He was only twenty and he had lost the person he loved most.

George Washington not only loved Lawrence, he respected him. Lawrence had been an officer in the militia. (A militia is a group of part-time soldiers who are not part of a regular army.) Now Lawrence's post was open. George took his brother's place.

A MILITIA MAN

Chapter 3
A Young Soldier

George,
Age 25

It was the early 1750s. For some time, France and England had been fighting over land in the Ohio River Valley. The problem was simple: Both countries wanted to control it.

The French built many forts in the area. They wanted to keep British colonists hemmed in on the east coast. George Washington was sent to deliver a warning to the French: Abandon the forts at once.

The French ignored the message. Still, the trip was an important one for George. Along with a small band of men, he traveled through a thousand miles of wilderness. He crossed two ranges of mountains. He got thrown off a crude raft into an icy river. The water was so cold, his clothes froze solid. Yet he made it home safely and was promoted for his bravery. He wrote a journal about his travels that appeared in newspapers. *The Journal of Major George Washington* made him famous.

In 1754 Benjamin Franklin drew this to urge colonists to unite to fight the French.

A few months later, he was sent back to the Ohio River Valley. This time there were more than a hundred and fifty men with him. They were to build a fort.

The British and French were not openly at war. But when Washington's men came upon French soldiers, a shot rang out. Which side began the attack? To this day, no one is sure who started it. But while Washington lost none of his men, ten French soldiers ended up dead. Among them was their leader.

That was all it took to spark a real war between the French and British. Soon eight hundred French soldiers along with four hundred Indians attacked Washington's much smaller army. A hundred of his men died. What choice did he have except to surrender? He and his men were not taken prisoner. Instead, they had to abandon their fort and return home.

For George, the defeat was a big blow. All his

life, he was concerned about his image. He wanted to appear brave, honorable. To surrender was embarrassing. Yet once again he was praised for his leadership. His career as a soldier was taking off.

Next he became the aide of the British general in charge of chasing out the French from the Ohio Valley. Up to now, Washington had led American soldiers. Now he was to serve alongside the tough, fearsome "redcoats." (This was the nickname for soldiers in the British army because of the bright red coats they wore.) The general assembled a mighty force of two thousand men to attack one of the largest French forts.

A Redcoat Soldier

In Europe, enemy armies met face-to-face, in open fields. Line after line of troops would march straight toward one another, firing cannons and muskets.

Washington warned the British general that fighting was done differently in America. The

A TYPICAL BATTLE IN EUROPE

trees

trees

rock

trees

British Troops

Enemy Troops

enemy would come at the redcoats from all sides. The French and Indians would attack from the woods. They would stay hidden behind trees and rocks.

The general refused to listen. The redcoats were to attack as they had been trained to. The result

A TYPICAL BATTLE IN AMERICA

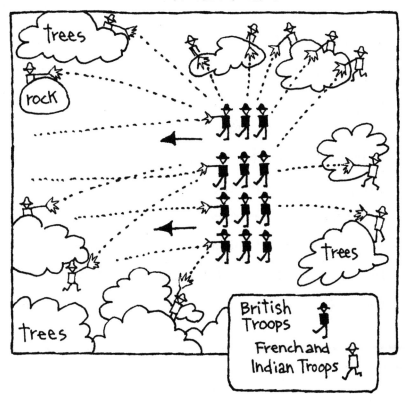

trees

rock

trees

trees

British Troops

French and Indian Troops

was a crushing disaster for the British. Soldiers on horseback were mowed down by hidden French and Indian forces. Soon hundreds of redcoats lay dead.

As for Washington, four musket shots tore through his coat. His hat was shot off his head. Two horses were shot from under him. Yet he was never hit.

The general was not so lucky. He died from a battle wound. So George Washington took command of all the frontier forces. He was only twenty-two years old. For five years, he helped build more than eighty forts in the Ohio River Valley. For five years, he fought against French troops as well as hostile bands of Indians.

In the end, the British won what became known as the French and Indian War. Colonists were now free to move west and settle the rich lands of the Ohio River Valley.

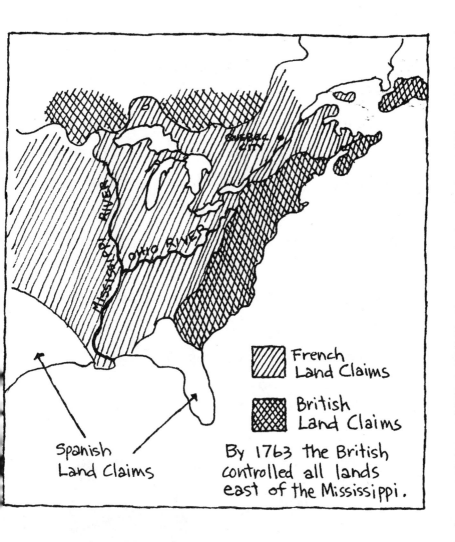

French
Land Claims

British
Land Claims

Spanish
Land Claims

By 1763 the British
controlled all lands
east of the Mississippi.

Chapter 4
Country Life

George had seen enough of war. He gave up his command and returned to Virginia. His brother Lawrence's wife had died. She had no living children. So Mount Vernon now belonged to George. He intended to live there peacefully for the rest of his life.

At a dance George met a very rich young widow with two young children. Her name was Martha Custis.

Martha Custis, 1757

She was short and plump with a warm smile. She knew the same people George knew. They both wanted the same kind of country life. In all ways it was a good match. "I have found an agreeable partner," he wrote to a friend.

On January 6, 1759, they were married. They both were twenty-seven years old. Although never wildly in love, there was a strong bond between them. Martha called George "Old Man" or "Papa." Sadly, they had no children together. But he doted upon little Patsy and her older brother Jacky.

PATSY AND JACKY

JACKY CUSTIS WAS FOUR AND HIS YOUNGER SISTER, PATSY, WAS TWO WHEN THEIR MOTHER MARRIED GEORGE WASHINGTON. GEORGE WAS GOOD TO HIS STEPCHILDREN. HE ORDERED FINE CLOTHES AND TOYS FOR THEM FROM ENGLAND. (GEORGE WAS VERY UPSET WHEN A DOLL FOR PATSY DIDN'T ARRIVE ON TIME.)

PATSY WAS A SWEET GIRL. FROM THE TIME SHE WAS VERY YOUNG SHE HAD SEIZURES, WHICH GREW WORSE AS SHE GOT OLDER. DOCTORS HAD NO IDEA HOW TO HELP HER. SHE DIED AFTER A SEIZURE WHEN SHE WAS ONLY SEVENTEEN.

JACKY WAS A SPOILED AND LAZY BOY. ALL HE WANTED WAS TO HAVE FUN. HE LASTED ONLY A FEW MONTHS AT COLLEGE IN NEW YORK BEFORE COMING HOME.

PATSY

HE WAS A FAILURE
AS A FARMER AND
DIED AT TWENTY-SIX,
JUST WEEKS AFTER
HIS STEPFATHER'S
ARMY WON THE WAR
FOR INDEPENDENCE.
JACKY'S SON AND
DAUGHTER WERE
RAISED AT MOUNT
VERNON BY GEORGE
AND MARTHA. (JACKY'S
WIFE AND TWO OLDER

JACKY

DAUGHTERS LIVED NEARBY IN VIRGINIA.)

AS FOR WHY GEORGE WASHINGTON HAD NO
FAMILY OF HIS OWN, MANY HISTORIANS THINK
SMALLPOX LEFT HIM UNABLE TO HAVE CHILDREN.

Both George and Martha loved to entertain. When he was a much older man, he claimed he and Martha hadn't dined alone in twenty years! Nearly every week company stayed over at Mount Vernon.

Washington was a most considerate host. One guest with a bad cold reported waking up in the night. There in his room stood George Washington with a hot cup of tea for him.

Martha Washington in middle age

George and Sweetlips at Mount Vernon

Two or three times a week, Washington went fox hunting. (One of his hunting dogs was named Sweetlips.) He liked to play cards and gamble for small sums of money. He'd meet up with friends at the local tavern to hear the latest gossip and jokes.

But running a large farm was serious business. It took up almost all his time. Washington rose early and had tea and pancakes with honey for breakfast. (The pancakes were cut into small slices, which made it easier for him to eat.) Then he would get on his horse and cover all four corners of his farmland. He helped drive the cattle and mend fences.

At first the farm raised and sold tobacco. Tobacco was difficult to grow even though Washington experimented with ways to improve his crop.

Tobacco

Later on he switched to growing wheat and built a mill to turn the wheat into flour. Wheat was much easier to grow and he could sell it locally whereas most of the tobacco was shipped to England.

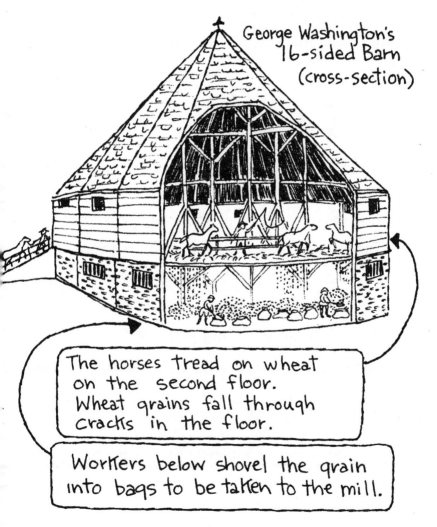

George Washington's 16-sided Barn (cross-section)

The horses tread on wheat on the second floor. Wheat grains fall through cracks in the floor.

Workers below shovel the grain into bags to be taken to the mill.

There were no grocery stores or clothing stores in the Virginia countryside. Expensive things like carriages and fancy clothes were shipped over from England. Almost everything else was grown or made on the farm. Linen for clothes was spun and woven there. Wool came from Mount Vernon sheep.

At Mount Vernon there were many people to feed and clothe. Between them, George and Martha owned as many as three hundred slaves. Like other rich farmers in the South, Washington had slaves grow his crops and work his fields. Later in life he began to see slavery for what it was—evil, cruel, and unjust. But for a long time he accepted slavery as just the way things were. He was neither a very harsh nor very kind master.

During his fifteen years as a farmer, George Washington was also an elected member of Virginia's House of Burgesses. The burgesses were men who met in Williamsburg. It was the capital

George Washington oversees his slaves.

of the colony then. They voted on local issues.

Even though the thirteen colonies belonged to England, they each had some form of self-government. As long as the king and Parliament (the government in England) acted in the colonists'

SLAVERY

SLAVERY IN AMERICA BEGAN IN THE EARLY 1600S. IN THE 1750S, SLAVERY WAS STILL LEGAL IN ALL THIRTEEN COLONIES. HOWEVER, THERE WERE VERY FEW SLAVES IN THE NORTH. THE VAST MAJORITY OF SLAVES BELONGED TO LANDOWNERS IN VIRGINIA, SOUTH CAROLINA, AND GEORGIA.

WHY?

IN THE NORTH, THERE WASN'T THAT MUCH FERTILE SOIL. NO "CASH CROPS" (CROPS TO SELL), SUCH AS TOBACCO OR RICE OR COTTON, WERE GROWN AS WERE GROWN IN THE SOUTH. FARMERS MOSTLY OWNED SMALL PLOTS OF LAND. ONE FAMILY COULD MANAGE ALL THE WORK WITHOUT "EXTRA HANDS."

IN THE SOUTH, THOUGH, SOME FARMS (OR PLANTATIONS) STRETCHED FOR THOUSANDS OF ACRES. THEY GREW CROPS FOR PROFIT. MANY PEOPLE WERE NEEDED TO WORK THE FIELDS AND GET THE CROPS TO MARKET. SLAVES WERE THE CHEAPEST SOURCE OF LABOR: THEY RECEIVED NO PAY. KIDNAPPED FROM AFRICA AND SOLD AT AUCTIONS, SLAVES HAD NO RIGHTS. THEY WERE THE PROPERTY OF THEIR MASTER, JUST LIKE A PLOW OR A HORSE. BESIDES GEORGE WASHINGTON,

A Slave Auction

THOMAS JEFFERSON WAS ALSO A SLAVE OWNER. IN HIS WILL, GEORGE WASHINGTON STATED THAT ALL HIS SLAVES WERE TO BE FREED AFTER MARTHA'S DEATH. HOWEVER, HE NEVER FREED ANY OF THEM WHILE HE WAS ALIVE.

MANY NORTHERN COLONIES OUTLAWED SLAVERY BY THE LATE 1700S. BUT IT TOOK THE CIVIL WAR (1861-1865) TO END SLAVERY IN THE SOUTH FOR GOOD.

interests, it was a pretty good arrangement. Most colonists were proud to be British subjects.

Then in the 1760s, the situation changed.

DON'T TREAD ON ME

This flag symbolized colonial defiance.

Chapter 5
Breaking Away

The long French and Indian War had been very costly for England. The king—George II—had borrowed a lot of money. The war had been fought on American soil. Even after England won, an army of ten thousand redcoats remained in America in case the French acted up again.

In 1763 the king's grandson—George III—took

King George III of England

the throne. The new king thought it only fair for the colonies to pay for the war expenses. Where would the money come from?

Taxes.

In 1765 the English Parliament passed the Stamp Act. In the colonies, all kinds of documents and paper goods suddenly had to carry a stamp on them. Wills, contracts, college diplomas, and marriage licenses weren't valid without the stamp. Newspapers and playing cards had to be stamped, too. The stamps didn't cost much. But the colonists were furious.

It was one thing for their own local governments to pass new taxes. Local governments were made up of men elected by the colonists. But Parliament was three thousand miles away. Colonists had no power there. They hadn't elected any of the members of Parliament. Nor could they vote them out of office.

What seemed fair to the king and to Parliament

Burning stamps in protest in New York

on one side of the Atlantic seemed totally unfair to colonists in America.

Where did George Washington stand on the Stamp Act?

He thought it was wrong, but he didn't join in the protests.

Parliament ended the Stamp Act in 1766 because so many angry colonists had stopped buying British goods. It was hurting trade. But the very next year Parliament forced colonists to pay taxes on paper, paint, glass, lead, and tea. All these items were imported from England.

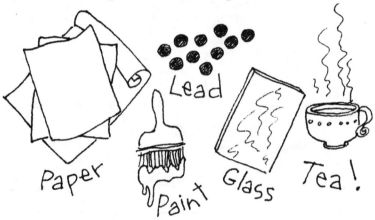

Once again protests in America brought about the repeal—the end—of the taxes, all except for one: The tax on tea.

A tax on tea may not seem important. But tea was a very popular drink in the colonies. People often drank fifteen cups a day. Taxing tea made everyone mad . . . including George Washington. Rather than pay the tea tax, he switched to coffee.

The latest round of taxes changed his feelings about being an English subject. He thought Parliament's control of the colonies was unjust. It had to stop. He wrote to a friend that colonists should not "hesitate to use arms" to defend their rights.

Before the wave of taxes, the thirteen colonies had little in common with one another. Each colony considered itself a separate land with its own separate interests.

Now anger over taxes brought the colonies together. It united them.

England cracked down on Boston after the Tea Party. The harbor was closed. The local government was shut down. British troops moved in. No goods could come in or go out of the city. Business came to a halt. Food was scarce. Still, the citizens

BOSTON TEA PARTY

IN NEW YORK AND PHILADELPHIA ANGRY CROWDS
PREVENTED BRITISH BOATS FROM UNLOADING
CARGOES OF TEA.

ON THE NIGHT OF DECEMBER 16, 1773, MEN IN BOSTON WENT EVEN FURTHER. THEY BELONGED TO A GROUP CALLED THE SONS OF LIBERTY. DRESSED AS MOHAWK INDIANS, THEY SNEAKED ONTO THREE SHIPS AND DUMPED 342 CHESTS OF TEA INTO THE HARBOR.

THE EVENT BECAME KNOWN AS THE BOSTON TEA PARTY. KING GEORGE III WAS FURIOUS! HE THOUGHT THE COLONISTS SHOULD HAVE TO PAY FOR THE TEA—AND THAT THEY HAD TO BE PUNISHED!

refused to pay for the ruined tea. After all, they had only been standing up for their rights.

People in other colonies sided with Boston, including George Washington. That summer, a meeting among the colonies took place in Philadelphia. George Washington was one of six men from Virginia who attended.

The Continental Congress, as it was called, represented twelve of the colonies. (Georgia decided not to come.) Nobody talked about breaking away from England, not yet. They still hoped the situation would improve.

But by the time the Second Continental Congress met in May 1775, the mood had

Independence Hall in Philadelphia

changed greatly. Fighting had already broken out between colonists and redcoats in a few Massachusetts towns. Americans had died. There was no turning back now. The colonies wanted independence!

The Second Continental Congress began to prepare for war. George Washington had arrived in

The Battle of Lexington

his blue soldier's jacket. He was forty-three now. He had been a farmer for the past fifteen years. As for his early war record, it was not great. He'd never won a field battle or ever commanded a large army.

Nevertheless, in June 1775 he was asked to lead the brand-new Continental Army. He said yes, though he had serious doubts as to his ability. His first reaction was to turn bright red, and then he ran out of the meeting!

THE DECLARATION OF INDEPENDENCE

GEORGE WASHINGTON HEADED THE SECOND CONTINENTAL CONGRESS IN PHILADELPHIA. HE SAT FACING THE OTHER DELEGATES WHO DISCUSSED PLANS FOR WAR. THOMAS JEFFERSON WAS ASKED TO WRITE DOWN ALL THE REASONS FOR BREAKING AWAY FROM ENGLAND. BEN FRANKLIN HELPED HIM, BUT THE WORDS ARE MOSTLY JEFFERSON'S. AND THEY ARE AMONG THE MOST FAMOUS WORDS IN ALL OF AMERICAN HISTORY.

THE DECLARATION OF INDEPENDENCE WAS SIGNED ON JULY 4, 1776, BY THE DELEGATES AT THE CONGRESS. ONE MAN, JOHN HANCOCK, WROTE HIS SIGNATURE IN HUGE BOLD LETTERS. TODAY IF SOMEONE ASKS FOR YOUR "JOHN HANCOCK," IT MEANS THEY WANT YOUR SIGNATURE.

Colonists in New York City
tore down a statue of
King George III.

Chapter 6
The Commanding General

General Washington, 1777

The War for Independence lasted from 1775 to 1783. Of course everyone knows how it ended: The colonists won the war. To us it doesn't seem as if it could have happened any other way. But during the war no one could be sure of the outcome. In fact, it seemed as if the colonists had very little chance against England.

The Continental Army that Washington led went into the war with no training. Soldiers were young, poor, and uneducated. Most were between fifteen and twenty-five years old. Most joined the army because few other choices were open to them. They wanted the pay.

There were never enough soldiers. The living conditions were terrible. (In fact, more American soldiers were killed by smallpox and other diseases than from battle wounds.)

Continental
Soldiers

There often wasn't enough ammunition, or food, or clothes. Soldiers went months without pay. And as the war dragged on year after year, George Washington found it harder and harder to get money for the army's needs.

Compared to British generals, George Washington knew little about waging war. (Before taking command of his troops, he bought five books that taught military tactics.) Indeed, out of nine battles he fought in, he only won three.

The enemy he faced was the mighty British army. It was the biggest and best-trained fighting machine in the world. The British navy owned the seas. British generals and admirals were brave and war-tested.

So how, against all odds, did the Americans win?

One reason is that they simply stuck it out.

George leads a retreat.

The longer the Continental Army hung in the war, the more likely it became that at some point the British would give up. In a way, the Americans didn't have to win. They just couldn't lose.

Over time, Washington became a shrewder general. He came to see that short, surprise strikes against the enemy were better than staging big battles. This wasn't considered a gentlemanly way to fight. (All his days, George Washington was concerned about his image.) But surprise attacks paid off.

The Continental Army was fighting for a cause. Americans wanted independence and were willing to die for it. They were also fighting on home turf. British soldiers, on the other hand, were in a strange place, three thousand miles from home. They were fighting only because it was their job.

In 1778, the French decided to help the

A Surprise Attack Near Princeton

AT VALLEY FORGE

1777–1778

George Washington

Marquis de Lafayette

Americans. (Britain, after all, was France's long-time enemy.) Besides money and ships, the French sent troops. Among them was a brave young nobleman, the Marquis de Lafayette. He became one of George Washington's closest, most trusted aides. He was almost like a son to Washington.

In 1778, a man arrived at the army's winter quarters in Valley Forge, Pennsylvania. He said he was a German general and called himself Baron von Steuben. He wasn't a general or a baron. But he had been a soldier since he was sixteen. He knew all about training soldiers.

Von Steuben taught Washington's men to work as a unit. He taught them to keep fighting even though they were afraid, even though friends were dying around them. Because of the baron, the Continental Army became much more professional. That helped win the war.

Baron
von Steuben

Perhaps, more important than anything else, George Washington was the reason for victory. Despite defeats, common soldiers always had faith in him. During the long war, four British commanding generals came and went. For the Americans, there was only one—Washington.

To everyone he was known as "His Excellency." Quiet and aloof, he was not chummy with his soldiers. He did not joke with them. But he always treated them with respect. He was a natural-born leader, and his men felt tremendous loyalty to him.

At times Washington seemed almost super-human. He never showed fear. The horror of war never affected his health or his outer calm. He'd play catch with his aides to relieve stress.

Indeed the pressure must have been tremendous. Men's lives were in his hands—and not just on the battlefield. One never-ending problem for Washington was not being able to

clothe and feed his soldiers properly. The Congress
in Philadelphia didn't have the power to supply
money or send more troops. And local governments in the colonies weren't eager to raise taxes to
fund what had become a very long war.

Washington saw the bigger picture. Yes, this
was a war for independence. But if the colonies
won freedom from England, what would hap-
pen then? Washington gave much thought to this
all during the war. If a new country was born,

he came to believe that it must have a strong central government. Just as his army needed a strong commanding officer, Washington believed that a new country, made from the different colonies, would need a strong leader. Not a king but an elected leader.

A British
Tax Stamp

Chapter 7
Hard Times

Most of the battles in the war were fought in New York, New Jersey, and Pennsylvania. In late fall of 1778, the Continental Army won an important victory in Saratoga, New York. After receiving the good news, Washington led ten thousand of his men westward in Pennsylvania. They would set up camp until spring, when

The British Surrender at Saratoga

battles would resume. He picked a place called Valley Forge. It was easy to defend. Also his spies could keep an eye on British troops in nearby Philadelphia.

The months at Valley Forge should have been a time for the troops to rest up, regain their strength. However, the weather turned bitter cold. The huts the soldiers built had no heat. (The snow made all the wood too damp to burn.)

In letters to the Continental Congress, Washington kept begging for help. He needed uniforms, shoes, and food. Washington was told to stop his "whining complaints."

How bad was it for the soldiers?

Many were dressed only in rags. Some had no clothes at all, just a tattered blanket. Sometimes a soldier had to borrow someone else's rags to go on duty. Officers who had shoes poured whiskey in them to prevent frostbite. Common soldiers often went barefoot. Washington reported seeing "blood

from their feet" in the snow. Some soldiers' frozen feet turned black and had to be amputated.

There was no food for the horses. Most fell down dead. There wasn't enough food for the soldiers, either. They would go for days without even so much as a bite of meat. They were near starvation.

As always, Martha came to stay with her husband and the troops at winter camp. Everyone called her Lady Washington. She couldn't stand the sight of blood and was known for saying that she shuddered at the sound of a gunshot. Yet she knew being there meant a lot to the soldiers as well as her husband. At Valley Forge, she cared for the sick and would leave small gifts for them. Still, a quarter of the troops (2,500) died from disease.

What is even more terrible is that the suffering at Valley Forge was unnecessary. Pennsylvania farmers had recently harvested their crops. It had been a very good year. They could have supplied the troops with food and clothes but chose instead to reap bigger profits by selling to the British.

Terrible as the time was at Valley Forge, conditions at the winter camp in Morristown the following year were worse. Soldiers were deserting. Sick soldiers were dying in huge numbers. Washington's army was down to eight thousand men, and of those, fewer than three thousand were well enough to fight.

More bad news came that summer. The city of Charleston, South Carolina, fell to the British. After that, there was an American defeat in Savannah, Georgia. And then in the fall, Washington learned that Benedict Arnold, a daring and trusted general,

had gone over to the British side. (Arnold did it for money, and to this day is considered the worst traitor in American history.)

Benedict Arnold

TORIES

LOOKING BACK TO A LONG-AGO TIME, IT IS EASY TO THINK THAT EVERYONE IN THE COLONIES WAS FIGHTING TOGETHER, THAT THEY ALL BELIEVED IN THE SAME CAUSE. BUT THAT ISN'T SO. NOT ALL AMERICANS SHARED IN "THE SPIRIT OF '76." JOHN ADAMS, WHO BECAME THE SECOND PRESIDENT, ESTIMATED THAT ONE THIRD OF COLONISTS WERE FOR INDEPENDENCE, ONE THIRD WANTED TO REMAIN BRITISH (THESE COLONISTS WERE CALLED TORIES), AND ONE THIRD DIDN'T CARE MUCH ONE WAY OR THE OTHER.

John
Adams

DURING THE WAR, MANY TORIES WERE PUNISHED
AS TRAITORS. SOMETIMES THEY WERE TARRED
AND FEATHERED—AFTER HOT TAR WAS POURED ON
THEM, THEY WERE COATED IN WHITE FEATHERS.
THEN THEY WERE HOISTED UP ON A RAIL AND
"RIDDEN" OUT OF TOWN.

AFTER THE WAR, MOST TORIES ENDED UP
MOVING TO CANADA OR SAILING BACK TO ENGLAND.

Chapter 8
Victory

George Washington,
Age 55

The Continental Army was in a shambles in the spring of 1781, yet only seven months later, the war ended.

One battle changed everything.

For a long time Washington had dreamed of retaking New York City, which had been captured by the British. Washington wanted a "big win" badly. But wisely, he now focused on victory in the South, in Virginia.

The British commanding general—Lord Charles Cornwallis—had just moved his entire army to Yorktown, Virginia. It was on a peninsula, which meant his army was surrounded on three sides by water.

As American ships headed into the area, a fleet of French ships joined them. Then Washington sent two thousand troops to join forces with French soldiers at the tip of the peninsula. All told, Washington had the strength of twenty-one thousand men; Cornwallis had only about seven thousand.

Cornwallis's army was not only outnumbered, it was hemmed in on all sides. The British were trapped!

The battle began. And on October 17, on the eighth day of bombardment, General Cornwallis surrendered. Two days later, George Washington sat on his favorite horse, Nelson, watching the defeated British soldiers march out of Yorktown.

THE BATTLE OF YORKTOWN 1781

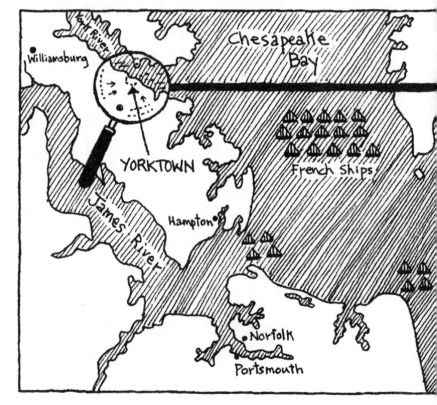

Williamsburg

Chesapeake Bay

YORKTOWN

French Ships

James River

Hampton

Norfolk

Portsmouth

He did not realize right then that this victory spelled the end of the war. But it had.

The Americans had won independence!

It took two years before a treaty between Britain and the United States was signed in Paris, France.

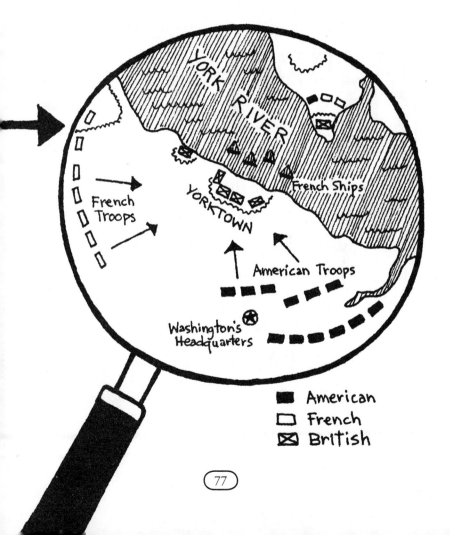

French Troops

YORK RIVER

French Ships

YORKTOWN

American Troops

Washington's Headquarters

■ American
☐ French
⊠ British

As soon as word of the treaty came, Washington said farewell to his army. First he said good-bye to the ordinary soldiers. He called them a "patriotic band of brothers." A month later he met with his officers in Fraunces Tavern, in New York City. (The tavern is still there.) He broke down in tears—here were men who had stood by him through the long years of war. Each officer stood before him for a handshake, then a kiss on the cheek.

George Washington resigned from the army. On Christmas Eve, 1783, he arrived home. Martha was there at Mount Vernon to greet him. He planned to take up farming again and spend the rest of his days in Virginia. He was fifty-one years old. It was time to retire.

THE TREATY OF PARIS

THE WAR ENDED IN OCTOBER 1781. THE TREATY OF PARIS WASN'T SIGNED UNTIL SEPTEMBER 1783. THE TREATY RECOGNIZED THAT THE UNITED STATES WAS A SEPARATE, FREE COUNTRY. THE BOUNDARIES OF THE NEW COUNTRY WOULD GO FROM THE GREAT LAKES AND MAINE TO FLORIDA, FROM THE ATLANTIC COAST TO THE MISSISSIPPI RIVER.

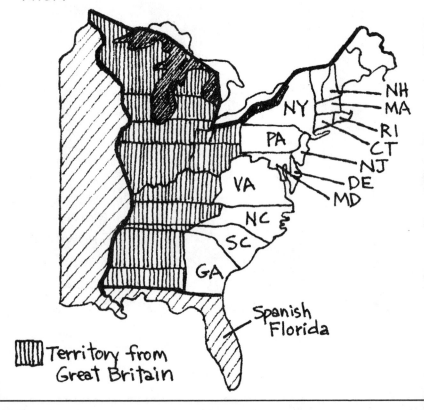

John Jay

John Adams

Benjamin Franklin

Henry Laurens

William Temple Franklin

A FAMOUS ARTIST OF THE TIME NAMED BENJAMIN WEST WAS TO PAINT A GROUP PORTRAIT OF THE BRITISH AND THE AMERICANS WHO SIGNED THE TREATY. THE PAINTING, HOWEVER, WAS NEVER FINISHED. ALTHOUGH THE AMERICANS (INCLUDING BENJAMIN FRANKLIN AND JOHN ADAMS) POSED FOR WEST, THE BRITISH REFUSED TO BE IN THE PICTURE.

Chapter 9
A Brand-New Country

George,
Age 58

George Washington was living again in his beloved Virginia. He was still the most famous man in America, just as he had been all through the war. A constant stream of visitors arrived at Mount Vernon. Everyone wanted to meet "His Excellency."

What brought Washington out of retirement?

George and Martha at home with two of their grandchildren

The country was floundering. The government was weak. It didn't have the power to raise taxes or control trade or mark state boundaries.

Washington said it was "as clear to me as the ABC," that the new country needed a much stronger system. In 1787, at a convention held in Philadelphia, the Constitution was written. It mapped out the kind of government George

THE CONSTITUTIONAL CONVENTION

Washington hoped for. There would be three branches of power—a strong president, a Congress to pass laws, and a Supreme Court to rule on whether laws were fair. No one branch would have too much power.

Even before the first election for president was held, everyone knew George Washington would win.

The election system then was different from the way it is now. Electors from the different states were chosen. Each had two votes. Everyone voted for Washington. So he became president. John Adams came in second, with thirty-four votes. So he became vice president.

George Washington received the news on April 14, 1789. Two days later he set out for

Federal Hall in New York City

the temporary capital, New York City. There he would take the oath of office. He said there were no "words to express" how anxious he felt. He was walking "on untrodden ground." He meant there was no path for him to follow, because no one had ever been president before.

front

back

Buttons commemorating George Washington's presidency

George Washington was sworn in on a balcony
at Federal Hall. He said, "I do solemnly swear that
I will faithfully execute the office of President of

the United States, and will to the best of my ability, preserve, protect and defend the Constitution of the United States." Every U.S. president has taken the same oath.

No one even knew what to call the president. John Adams suggested "His Elective Highness." Others suggested "His Mightiness" or "Majesty." Washington didn't like anything that sounded as if he were a king. In the end he decided "Mr. President" would do just fine.

The job of president is still in many ways what George Washington first made of it. The president is in charge of foreign policy. That means how the United States deals with other countries. The president presents a budget to Congress, asking for money to run the government. The president is commander in chief of the army. The president chooses a cabinet, people to advise him on important issues.

The president also appoints judges, including

judges on the Supreme Court who serve for life. (When a Supreme Court judge dies, resigns, or retires a new one is then appointed.)

WASHINGTON'S CABINET

Secretary of the Treasury, Alexander Hamilton

Secretary of State, Thomas Jefferson

Secretary of War, Henry Knox

Attorney General, Edmund Randolph

George, Age 66

When his first four-year term was over in 1793, Washington was ready to retire. He was in his sixties. His hair had turned white. His teeth hurt worse than ever. Recently he'd come down with pneumonia.

But the country was still so new and frail. Thomas Jefferson and others wanted Washington to stay on for another four years. The United States would be a little older then, and stronger.

When the electors cast their votes, again Washington won. And again John Adams came in second.

Washington's second term as president was an unhappy one, almost right from the start.

There was a short-lived rebellion of farmers. They rose up because they didn't want to pay certain taxes on corn.

Angry farmers attack a tax collector.

Washington also agreed to a new treaty with the British. It made him very unpopular. But he wanted to avoid another war with the British while the country was still going through "growing pains." One newspaper went so far as to call Washington a fake patriot, a hypocrite. The personal insults hurt him greatly.

The only part of his job that Washington took pleasure in was planning the new capital. There first had been a capital in New York, then in Philadelphia. This one would be permanent. Not far from Mount Vernon, it was called Washington City. He saw to the building of the new president's house. Sadly, he is the only president who never got to live in the White House.

PLANS FOR THE NEW CAPITAL,
WASHINGTON, D.C.

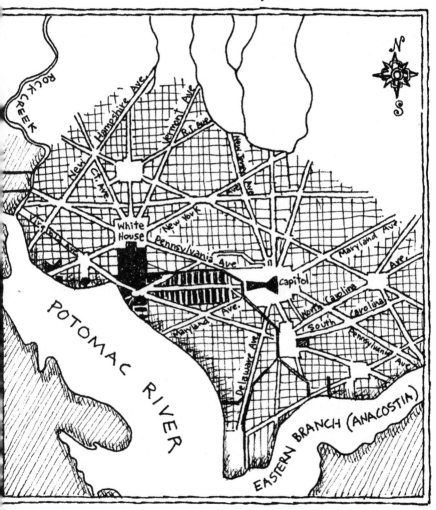

James Hoban, an Irishman living in Charleston, South Carolina, won the White House design contest judged by George Washington.

By the time his second term as president was nearly over, Washington was bound and determined to leave government. He wrote a "farewell address" printed in newspapers across the country. He thought two terms was long enough to serve as president. It was important to hand over power to the next president. That's what happens in a republic. King George III had once said that if Washington chose to give up power, "he'd be the greatest man on earth."

That's exactly what he did.

For the third and last time, he retired. Sadly he didn't enjoy the peace of Mount Vernon for very long. December 12, 1799, was a cold, rainy day. As usual, Washington came home after many hours of farmwork. He didn't bother to change his wet clothes before dinner. Two days later, he developed a bad throat infection. "I find myself going," he whispered to Martha. Then after taking his own pulse, George Washington died. He was sixty-seven years old.

George on his deathbed

The Washington Family Tomb

Martha insisted on a simple funeral and burial at Mount Vernon. However, across the country there were tributes to George Washington. People felt a terrible loss. It almost seemed impossible to think of the young United States without George Washington.

Right away Congress began talking of building a monument to him. (No building in Washington, D.C., can be taller than the Washington Monument, which was finished in 1880.) And a national holiday in February celebrates George Washington's birthday.

THE
WASHINGTON
MONUMENT

When it was built, this was the tallest man-made structure in the world.

MOUNT RUSHMORE

George Washington
Thomas Jefferson
Theodore Roosevelt
Abraham Lincoln

The faces carved on Mount Rushmore in South Dakota were the work of Gutzon Borglum and took fourteen years to complete.

George Washington is so famous that sometimes he seems more like a monument than a flesh-and-blood man. We think of him as the face on dollar bills and quarters.

Yet he was as human as anybody. He lived through amazing times and left his mark on our country in a way that no one else has. Perhaps the best tribute came from another signer of the Declaration of Independence, Harry Lee, who praised "the memory of the Man, first in war, first in peace, and first in the hearts of his country-men."

TIMELINE OF
GEORGE WASHINGTON'S LIFE

1732	George is born February 22
1746	George moves to Mount Vernon
1752	George's brother, Lawrence, dies
1754	George is a lieutenant colonel during the French and Indian War
1759	George marries Martha Dandridge Custis on January 6
1773	Martha's daughter, Patsy, dies at the age of 17
1775	The American Revolution begins and George takes command of the Continental Army; the Second Continental Congress meets
1776	George signs the Declaration of Independence
1777	Winter at Valley Forge, Pennsylvania
1781	Martha's son, Jacky, dies at the age of 26
1783	The American Revolution ends
1787	George is present at the Philadelphia Convention for the drafting of the United States Constitution
1789	George becomes the first president of the United States
1792	George is reelected as president
1797	George retires to Mount Vernon
1799	George dies December 14 at the age of 67, at Mount Vernon
1802	Martha Washington dies May 22 at the age of 71, at Mount Vernon

TIMELINE OF THE WORLD

Benjamin Franklin discovers the electrical nature of lightning and invents the lightning rod	1752
The French and Indian War begins in America	1754
George III takes the throne in England	1760
English Parliament passes the Stamp Act	1765
The first paved sidewalk is laid in London, England	1766
Boston Tea Party	1773
Louis XVI becomes king of France	1774
The American Revolution begins	1775
The city of San Francisco is founded	1776
The French decide to help the Americans defeat the British	1778
Washington's victory at Yorktown brings about the end of fighting in the American Revolution	1781
The first parachute is demonstrated	1783
The French Revolution begins; soon there are widespread executions of French aristocrats	1789
Construction of the White House begins	1792
King Louis XVI and his wife, Marie Antoinette, are beheaded	1793
John Adams becomes president of the United States; Thomas Jefferson is vice president	1797

BIBLIOGRAPHY

Buller, Jon, et al. **Smart about the Presidents.** Grosset & Dunlap, New York, 2004.

Calkhoven, Laurie. **George Washington: An American Life.** Sterling Publishing Company, New York, 2006.

Jurmain, Suzanne Tripp. **George Did It.** Dutton Children's Books, New York, 2006.

Krull, Kathleen. **Lives of the Presidents.** Harcourt Trade, California, 1998.

Marrin, Albert. **George Washington & the Founding of a Nation.** Dutton Children's Books, New York, 2001.